Seeing Birds in Church is a Kind of Adieu

ARLENE ANG

Published by Cinnamon Press
Meirion House, Glan yr afon, Tanygrisiau, Blaenau Ffestiniog
Gwynedd, LL41 3SU
www.cinnamonpress.com

The right of Arlene Ang to be identified as author of this work has been asserted by her in accordance with the Copyright, Designs and Patent Act, 1988. Copyright © 2010 Arlene Ang
ISBN: 978-1-907090-06-6
British Library Cataloguing in Publication Data. A CIP record for this book can be obtained from the British Library.
All rights reserved. No part of this publication may be reproduced, stored in a retrieval system, or transmitted in any form or by any means, electronic, mechanical, photocopying, recording or otherwise without either the prior written permission of the publishers. This book may not be lent, hired out, resold or otherwise disposed of by way of trade in any form of binding or cover other than that in which it is published, without the prior consent of the publishers.

Designed and typeset in Palatino by Cinnamon Press. Cover design by Mike Fortune-Wood from original artwork 'Lullaby' by Oana Cambrea (cutteroz.carbonmade.com) Printed in Poland.. Cinnamon Press is represented in the UK by Inpress Ltd www.inpressbooks.co.uk and in Wales by the Welsh Books Council www.cllc.org.uk.

Acknowledgements

Grateful acknowledgement is made to the editors of the following publications where some of these poems, at times in their earlier versions, first appeared: *Astropoetica, Boxcar Poetry Review, Contemporary American Voices, Dandelion, Eclectica, Envoi, FRiGG, Ink and Ashes, Ghoti Magazine, Mimesis, Obsessed with Pipework, Orbis, Other Voices International Project, The New Imagist, Pebble Lake Review, Pemmican, Poetry Ireland, (poetry) WORM, The Potomac, Radiant Turnstile, Seam, The SHOp, Smiths Knoll, Stirring, Umbrella, Wicked Alice.*

Special thanks to Ros Barber and Merryn Williams for their inspiring sonnets as well as to the kind editors of *Modern Poetry in Translation* for the use of Jean Cassou's lines in Jacqueline Kiang's beautiful rendition of his sonnets.

Contents

A Sun That Isn't a Source of Heat	7
Fishbowl	8
Underworld	10
What the Tabby Scratched Today	11
Surface	12
Crucifixion	13
One	14
Franklin in the Garden	15
The Weight of Seasons	16
Col San Martino	17
Ducks release concentric circles	18
Window Screen	20
Cordon Bleu	22
Parco San Lazzaro	23
Not So Much the Dark	24
Night, with Owls on Witch Trees	25
Love Letter	26
In Memoriam	27
Ghost	28
Fallen	29
The Bearded Lady	30
Abandoned	31
Shelter	32
Bringing the Body Home	33
Driver Looking Back	34
Drink	35
Rain and Window-Gazing	36
Of Numbers and Nine Lives	37
The Astronomer's Last Nights	38
The heart stops momentarily	39
Dead Girl Found Curled Up in Snow	40

A Study of Loss	42
Dream Experiments Involving Polaroids	44
Glove Stories	45
Pandora	48
Seeing Birds in Church is a Kind of Adieu	52
Refraction	53
Inevitably	54
Something Like Blood	55
Seasonal Craving	56
This is not the poem	57
Ant trails	58
Insomnia	59
Approaching Death	60
Single Hung Window	61
Immortality	62
And Why Shouldn't I Cry Over Seinfeld?	63
In My Mother's Fridge	64
I won't ask you again	65
Surviving Grandfather	66
This is not the first time you tasted sand	67
5:37 p.m.	68
The Day She Was Called to Identify the Body	69
As we think	70
Hot tubs	72
Leopold's Room	73
The Ventriloquist Returns	74
Dollhouse	76
Winter Elements	77
Mrs D's Last Letter to Her Son	78
Death in the Afternoon	79
This closing book	80

Seeing Birds in Church is a Kind of Adieu

for my parents

A Sun That Isn't a Source of Heat But Instead Paints Its Grief on the Walls of a Private Room

The mirror is a lesson in stillness, in watching the room
as it takes place behind your left shoulder.

Like a mother, the clock wipes its face over and over
with its hands.

The wine glass in one of the paintings now appears
to the right of the bird with the broken wing.

A stray wind sucks the curtains into a perverse tango.

You watch a rat occupy that portion of the room
where you were told to sit and have a drink.

There is another hand, scarred where an extra finger
was surgically removed.

Dusk leads the sun away for its own good.

Candles are lit to represent soul and the burning
of material effects.

Now the hand is brushing the hair of a dead woman
into some semblance of order.

Or beauty.

Fishbowl

With her husband dead a fortnight,
Sadie emptied it. We don't ask where

she took the goldfish. The linoleum
collects us—the way an eye,

pupil dilated, gathers tears
and constructs its layer of cataract.

Instead of the mermaid,
there's his teeth—taken apart,

then glued together. Is the plastic
seaweed aware it is standing

on human ash? We don't
exactly know why we're here.

The doilies are punishing
the sideboard with floral designs.

Sadie recounts how he sank first
before floating back to the surface.

The chandelier has two bulbs
flickering a heartbeat against the walls.

With the brocade curtains drawn,
there's no looking out.

Sadie passes a tray of tuna
sandwiches around. No one asks

why she's wearing his clothes
upside-down. The sun is never

the same in any painting. There are
three waterscapes in the room:

one with a fish, one without
a fish, and one with nothing at all.

Underworld

It takes a minute to climb the roof.
The ladder is spiked with splinters that waylay
the hands. Once at the top,
you use your teeth to extract them from your skin.
The gathering dusk squeezes
the farmhouse into another world.
Ten yards out,
an abandoned forklift becomes an object
someone else is seeing
for the last time. If you could suck
the sting from your fingers,
would you have done the same
for your mother? A shingle
chooses to fall. The hens lift a squall of dust
in their search for worms. Silence itself
is a condition in which there's no longer anyone
telling you to come down because
you could hurt yourself. An hour quickly
turns to three. Like mosquitoes
on your bare arms. There's no rush now.
You watch the darkness settle
around the weeds drinking from the roots
of an oak. The child is no longer
part of the body, the pain that birthed him.
In your pocket, a chocolate coin reverts to its liquid
state and stains your trousers like nosebleed.

What the Tabby Scratched Today

The lampshade on the end table
is crooked. In the room, there are
signs of violence: a spilt vase,
the flowers crushed by fallen
books, the torn curtain, blood
on the sofa, animal fur on the rug.

My skirt is frayed at the hem,
the sole of my left boot threatens
to come off. The lights have gone out
the way a chameleon's tongue
furls back into its mouth.

A door flaps; this house has bats.
On my mother's desk, there's an old
Gratta e Vinci ticket. The price,
2500 lire, is half-covered by socks
she failed to mend. A black Labrador
licks its wounds by the dying fire.

Surface

The house grows out of the ground
like a head. Even its porch is an exercise

in attachment. The sun is drowning,
and takes half of the nailed floorboards

down with it. The windows appear
to sink in the tall grass. Someone is crying

because the sprinkler hasn't
turned itself on. The wooden bench

creaks as it sags under the weight of a body.
Old water rings from glasses

overlap on the armrests, like balloons
for the dead or fish faces. The husband,

in leaving, carries away a sheaf
of love poetry. The screen door howls

itself white in the corner of his eye.
With wild hands, he is feeling up his lost wife

in another woman, in another translation
of Apollinaire—the way a projector beams

scratchy images on a blank wall.
There is permanence in the structure

of the porch, but little else in the dead robin
left to gather maggots into its breast.

Crucifixion

In my father's studio,
there is no way to tell time.
Here he is painting his 111th crucifixion.
He starts with a graphite pencil.
He outlines a crescent
for where he'll lay Christ's head
and tiny holes for where the wounds
should go. The placement
of the nails could change anytime.
In this instant, he is asking
his dead boy why they must hide
from each other. He is asking,
*What was ever solved
by leaving?* Every three a.m.
he wakes up, and the suffering is different.
He could make the crown of thorns
appear larger than the body.
Or feed the wooden cross to termites.
Today he is having a hard time
with Christ's hands. He can't breathe.
He is powerless where it matters
most. Like today—
when he pries the window open,
and the glass breaks.

One

The wheelchair restructures the landscape
outside the window. One's neck movements

cause the steel handrims to plant a glimmer
in one's eyes. A blink is a practice in flinching.

One tends to forget, prefer absence to faces.
Easier than to watch the leg on the bed

by virtue of it sweating. Loss can smash
a water pitcher against the wall and leave

the carpet to absorb the orange juice,
the flies. *One must be patient*, says the doctor.

*It may take weeks to process your artificial
one. If one has no friends to talk to,*

I can recommend someone. He tilts his head
for confirmation and, in doing so, appears

to have hung himself with his stethoscope.
One has no more answers. One is tired

of holding one's body up for a weight that used
to be divisible by two. The doctor goes out

as quietly as he cut through bone and leaves
one to study the universe of one limb, missing.

Franklin in the Garden

He never mowed grass, he cut it.
The scissors, green-stained and rusted
to the quick, lay flat on the ground,
like ears listening for moles.
Every snip, he said, was his body
inching closer to that woman
with the blue parasol across the street.
And sometimes he thought of the mob
before the guillotine. He spoke
French to gardenias, to weeds
around the stone path where
the blades moved over like
gnarled hands. Afterwards,
he gathered grass in a black bag
and called the garbage collectors
by astrological sign. This was
how he learned to let it all go:
dates on the calendar, the current war,
St. Faustine's Hospice, his wife
in bed—her mouth partly open
to receive that last breath.

The Weight of Seasons

Dust paralyses the corridors
that branch out to different rooms—
the house a dead end of sorts.
The daily boy hurls newspaper into mud,
dog puddles. I remove the outer pages
like wilted lettuce leaves
until only the obituaries remain.

The dead refuse to be buried.
The attic creaks under the burden
of Grandmother's skillet, bric-a-brac
from relatives, the hunting gear
of various men, and children's toys
left on the rocking chair
where Mother darned socks.

I tick off calendar numbers,
travel slowly from room to room,
lighten the load by tossing
scraps of poetry over my shoulder—
salt for the devil—leaving answers
on crossword puzzles like slime
trailed by a garden snail.

Col San Martino

This is where the small car chugs
to a stop. Rust erodes red paint,
the sheen swept away by rain.

Sun—a crushed orange—bleeds
through afternoon mist. 45 miles
away, he is writing a novel on snow
crystals; your sons have his eyes.

From this hillside, the vineyards
sprawl like cemeteries, grape
stalks crucified on white pales.

Distance is crossed in dreams: he is
never there. Like turtles, children
grow out of their house. Did you really
believe you came for the *prosecco*?

This is the place where an old woman
watches from her window. Silence
quivers your hands on the wheel.

The journey is over. You empty
your pockets on the front seat: old coins,
a bracelet, fridge notes, his birthstone.
There is no burden like unwanted things.

Ducks release concentric circles

across the lake. I throw them
stale bread; the crumbs speckle

the air like a squall. Inside
I am hollow as the deer skull

hanging in my father's study.
In the half-light, bone rediscovers

its sheen. There's no dusk
for his teeth in the sealed urn now—

or the geraniums, the shoes
transformed to ash. John Alleyne,

in a 1931 lecture, awakened
people to the possibility

of elevating one's body
through force of suggestion.

Mosquitoes when they come,
leave red hills on my skin.

Immune response
or levitation? I remember

my father banging his fist
on the table when he learned

something was wrong in his mind.
A question of forgetfulness.

He was terrorised by larvae—
unlike ducks, which feed

on what they find and fly
without power of thought.

Window Screen

The day is a shipwreck.
I know it by the way wind lashes

against the screen. The mess
I've made of the window

by simply ignoring to clean.
Dirt is now in the mesh,

like names etched
on a tree. I've come so far

as to answer the phone
in that booth

across the street
and receive no reply.

Just open-mouth
breathing. From this height,

the antennae outside
twist into crucifixes

for the unsung. The wind is
swiftly closing doors.

The bed has been subjected
to a camouflage of dust—

that, to my touch,
could have been scabs.

When I fall asleep,
my eyes leave wet rings

on the pillow
as if I've been crying

all along, away from myself.
And heard the house

being taken away
on the shoulders of men.

Cordon Bleu

Their mother called every night *cordon bleu*.
She drank. For as long as seven days, she managed
to hold down a job washing dishes, like nausea.
The Catholic nuns educated her well. They taught her
Agnus Dei—which means things could be worse.
Like an orphanage. She reads the newspaper
every day. She listens to the radio from upstairs.
What is the upper class, she wants to know, if not
sleeping on the top bunk? She lets her children
steal what they can from the world. She locks herself
in a one-room flat. They enter like cats, bringing in
slaughter. Her hand wrinkles their hair. She lets them
take their turns on the bunk bed. When she passes
out, the green parquet freezes her cheek with its kiss.

Parco San Lazzaro

When the gardener approaches
the pond, his shoes sink halfway in the silt.

It is no coincidence that he sees his face
in the water. Even the language of scales

begins with a glimmer: the trout
are dying. Their silver bellies—tipped

to the sun—are his habitat.
He brings them stale bread as if

it matters. It is a small park,
and live fishes are cheaper than oxygen

or pond filters. A cigarette
becomes his wife in one hand—

smoky aftertaste and ash.
With the other, he retrieves the dead

with a net. He has until late
morning to get them out. The bodies pile

up in the bucket behind him.
Children clap. Later, he leaves his catch

in a place private to cats. The eyes,
never closed but always unseeing,

accept the hunger of the living.

Not So Much the Dark

Years pass and still I fear burglars:
the courteous ones with skullcaps,
crowbars, ski masks, perhaps
a swastika mosaic on their sweaters.

Bedtime was early; I read *Mickey
Mouse* under the quilt with a penlight,
listened to the hoax of branches
at the window, curtain rustle.

Downstairs, my mother, on her rocking
chair, stroked the tabby on her lap.
Her voice through the door a thirst
of hisses: they're coming, they're coming.

It was wartime, the house only half
a woman and child. Nightly,
she left tea and biscuits in the kitchen,
hoping to slow one or two of them down.

Night, with Owls on Witch Trees

We never make love, but lie face up
as if we could float all the way to Andromeda.

The ceiling fan slashes shadows
into the oak armoire: a Jesus rib, quilted leaves,
a cusp from the Queen of Hearts.

We are bone-naked under flannel,
like too many positives shuffling into papers.

Outside, a car stalls. Mice scurry
through grass. The neighbour's girl fumbles
with keys, the hand brake, buttons.

In the headlight across the room,
we spool breaths, hold out for an x-ray of sky.

Love Letter

We walked around the junkyard and found it. There —
between an old shoe and a wedge of coloured glass. Three

dogs behind a fence snarled. In the end, what
did we know of hunger? We'd seen how a turkey could thaw

on the *Daily News* It was cheap paper, crinkled in parts,
as if it had taken a rainstorm into its folds. A strap

of gum held a corner shut. We pulled it out and read:
Today, another bombing. It was undated, no *dear*,

darling or *yours truly. I watched a boy and his skate-
board blow up. Will I see you again?* Then, a quote from Keats:

How quiet death is. Several words were spelt
wrong. We headed home: this was how the dead slept.

In Memoriam

A plastic tulip in a vase—it's red
like lipstick on your glass, the shoes you wore
when late for work—and bread crumbs on the floor:
the neighbour's tabby bristles to be fed.

My black suit has been washed and pressed, a thread
hangs from its sleeve: the funeral's at four;
last time we both forgot to lock the door.

Your garden pansies droop, a mouse lies dead
on our rattan bench. I dress, the dim
bulb in the room like walnut-coffin sky.
A button rolls away; I clutch the air.

The porch is bathed in sun, unlikely hymn
for cancelled spring. The floorboards creak on my
way out. Too tight, I feel old fabric tear.

Ghost

sonnenizio on a line from Ros Barber

No-one can see you now. You are unglued,
bereft of movement. Where did you come from
if not your body? It's still there, like a used-
car lot with no cars. You explore it

the way a yew tree taps into the sandbox
by shedding its leaves. The room uses a bed
to fill itself halfway. There you find
an IV needle weeping into the vein, and urine

as it snakes down a tube. You hear
a uniform echo of yourself from the ventilator.
Your eyes have locked down. Now the universe
is invisible to you. Footfalls bring in voices,

like newspapers. It could be you imagine
the drink in them—useless and with little meaning.

Fallen

sonnenizio on a line from Ros Barber

No-one can see you now. You are unglued—
the way foetal limbs are scraped out of the uterus.
A car door immobilises you. It is scorched,
peeled into a uniform of black. There's a mouth

somewhere breathing away its life. You are
three-fourths of your unit. The rest lies
spattered around, usurping the roadside.
A U-shaped metal bleeds your throat.

This morning you had a girlfriend,
you had a mission, you had two legs attached
to your body. You hear a radio crackle—
useless proof that there's someone

out there. Dying is a universe of its own.
Your eyes fill with sun. You close them now.

The Bearded Lady

sonnenizio on a line from Ros Barber

On a morning like any other, she wakes to find
a slit in the curtains unsheathing the sun
across the bed. She calls her cat, a summons
that reverts back to silence. As she rises,

she leaves her hair behind—dark brown
and curling on the dishevelled sheets.
She undresses. The half-light gives itself
to inspecting her body. She has lost her beard

and a chunk of left breast. She has only
just begun. She turns her head to the pillow
where she had laid to sleep a husband
and two dogs. And there, she finds

what she was made to find: the dead mouse,
a sheen of blood ripening its half-closed mouth.

Abandoned

sonnenizio on a line from Merryn Williams

The baby crying. Gulls and North Sea air.
A coffeehouse cedes its damp tables to customers.
On the radio, the latest ceasefire in Fallujah
and dead seals washing up on shores.
A crowd seizes the sidewalk for itself,
like physicians eager to contain a disease.
Muffled cars seep in and out the morning fog.

Even hunger is a kind of seizure. One hand
peels away the blanket. One conceals
the newborn's sex. One sees to pressing 999
for assistance. We study the scene from behind
a glass window as we seed martini olives
inside our mouths; our hands kept clean.
There's a woman, too. She slips away unseen.

Shelter

sonnenizio on a line from Merryn Williams

The baby crying. Gulls and North Sea air.
At her feet, ants seethe around an apple core.
Even the sun is bruised and cedes part
of itself to the clouds. The ferry blurs into a seed

in the horizon, before ceasing altogether
to exist. Wind rages a seizure through her hair.
How does rain perceive the act of falling?
The metal bench seeps its inherent chill down

her spine. She receives it with a calm known
to the recently deceased. On her lips, blood like
sealing wax. She holds the baby closer,
seeking her childhood. Overhead, birds recreate

a makeshift ceiling with their underbellies
as they shake their hunger at the sea.

Bringing the Body Home

sonnenizio on a line from Merryn Williams

The baby crying. Gulls and North Sea air.
Faces seared by salt. A lurch, and the ferry detaches
itself from the dock—the way a heartbeat ceases
to be sound. Flatline and seam of horizon.
On the deck, a pair of lovers receive
the wind, like deceit. A grocery bag bursts, rolling
four oranges to my feet. I could be a précis
of loss, a lung disease contained by lips
turning blue. I have a receipt for the body.
I have a box. And the baby, seeking to possess
an empty bottle with her mouth. Hunger conceives
the strangest toys. It would seem I am again
with child. Left behind, the ferry's wake seethes.
I stand where I am: Husband, deceased.

Driver Looking Back

sonnenizio on a line from Merryn Williams

The baby crying. Gulls and North Sea air.
Two pine-tree fresheners, seared through by sun,
flap from the rearview mirror. A seizure
of sorts. The woman in the backseat is made

real by the milk seeping through her blouse.
It is the tendency of an object of hunger,
when left unattended, to seek out the hunger.
Her body perceives itself as a means to feed

its young—the way a kite string is seized
by cedar needles and tangled. She unbuttons
her shirt to cede a breast to the grappling mouth.
Outside, the wharf receives the fog. The taximeter

flicks on, the numbers like all-seeing eyes.
Happy hours light up bars. The seamless sky.

Drink

sonnenizio on a line from Jean Cassou

Then I lost you, like so many other things
that attach themselves to the material universe—
the way a yew tree, in falling, disperses
robins to the sky. The night was uterine,
torn up by headlights and misused by rain.

You lay on the wrong side of the road—
a uniform of twisted metal, bones,
blood, urine. Your green car has gone beyond
the skeleton of its usefulness. I was behind
the wheel, bent like a kitchen utensil,
crying for the hole you left in the windshield.
All around, the slivers of euthanasia.

You opened your mouth, as if to swallow air.
Too late. The air had usurped your last breath.

Rain and Window-Gazing

sonnenizio on a line from Jean Cassou

If I drink at your sky it is because
I've been split by lightning. The asphalt
winks a submerged city. My clothes
are wet, and the grit in your eyes

films the wrong grief. Itinerant
cars swoosh the rain alive. It's late.
The rabbit's foot keychain in your pocket
mourns its lost body, like a map

of Italy. We are less than perfect,
unfit to collect fish from their happiness.
The slit in the horizon is an empty house.
We watch as shop mannequins, in vitro,

put on clouds. I sit inside this bird
bath and spirit your face from the rainwater.

Of Numbers and Nine Lives

These days the neighbour's cat sleeps on my chest;
I'm hollow as a spoon curved to ensnare
a taste of broth. My tongue uncurls a prayer:
I'm stainless now. The surgeon badly stressed:
Our time is short, expect the worst. I've messed
up half my kitchen and Mum's silverware,
failed breast exams, paid blindly with my hair.
Wall mirrors make me look away. Undressed,
I'm gauzed to ward off flies. The stand fan ticks
away my thoughts. I'm here just to survive.
Some days I feel allergic to the sound
of purrs, a warmth that makes me sneeze. It flicks
its tail against my nose. I count to five:
the years before another lump is found.

The Astronomer's Last Nights

The sky is a cobweb of stars;
frogs hop on the garden
path, their mating calls like sitars
with broken necks. It is ten
o'clock. Indoors, we calculate
his pills in scheduled charts,
the light-years before a prostate
turns supernova, the quarts
of water intake in one day.
Dust coats his telescope;
silence hangs in the Milky Way—
wisps of gas like expired hope:
the Witch's Broom Nebula gleams.
It's easy to forget
his notes on interstellar beams,
the radiance of sunset.
He sleeps, mindless of the rising pitch.
Like distant light, his hands twitch.

The heart stops momentarily

and grass bends to accommodate
the body's weight. A blue umbrella skips

away, like a sailboat ripped from
its anchor. The eyes fill up on rain,

tiny insects, and become transparent.
What is the feeling now of the wrist twitching

beneath the clasp of this amethyst
bracelet? Once blown off the skin, clothes

have no memory of wholeness.
In an interview, the woman who got struck

by lightning twice admitted
she never had any premonition of living.

Overhead, the birds are excited by
the sight of earthworms surfacing the soil.

Dead Girl Found Curled Up in Snow

She is an ear.
She is a sea shell

taken—like a taste
for destruction—

from the sea.
Her body

conforms
to the beauty

inherent in snow.
The needle

splitting the vein
on her arm

has fallen into
a trance.

Her fingers curve
gracefully—

as if halfway
into the interpretation

of *Claire de Lune*.
It is time

for her to leave.
She is nameless.

The ice holds
her blue lips together.

She doesn't wake up,
doesn't know

the hollowed womb
she's left

on the ground,
or later

how more snow fell
and erased all

trace of where
she didn't belong.

A Study of Loss

It becomes so that you doubt
the existence of fruit:

if you cut your finger
from a page in the Bible,

the wound will take the shape
of a blade; the gap

will fill up with blood.
What is the identity

of the fruit bowl once the fruit
has been taken from it?

Emptiness, they say,
is relative. When you look

in the mirror,
part of your body replaces

the wall's reflection:
the presence of one thing

obscures another.
The fruit bowl's strength lies

on its acceptance of loss.
During a solar eclipse,

the new moon has no notion
of passing in front

of the sun. Once the father
has left, his shoes

will remain unlaced
by the bed. Even all this waiting

is a kind of wake.
Death itself is a growing out

of one's body—
the way old fruit is discarded

from the bowl.
If you listen carefully,

you'll hear how the house
creaks from the burden

of holding itself together.

Dream Experiments Involving Polaroids

Before my mother goes to bed
bearing the extraction of her breast, she has
to walk away from me.
She keeps slipping on the floor.
She is halfway to saying
goodbye. Instead she turns around
and takes a snapshot
of my face looking in on her
from the French window. She slips again.
The nightdress climbs her hip
and shows the moon
all the veins where the blood went
wrong. She is weeping now.
The picture in her hand has captured
only the wedge of my red shoe.
In the next five hundred dream states,
she will explain to everyone
this is how much she loves me,
that I will always remain a living person to her.
The soundtrack is that of a body crossing
itself over and over. She has
no notion of how little they understand
what she says. It's been like this
every time: we meet, we fail
in our attempts to take photos of each other,
we don't talk, we don't go into details—
like which one of us is dead. Or isn't.

Glove Stories

i. Elaine

In slipping her hands
out of the gloves, she has admitted
the cold. Blue woollen lips,
half-open on the table—
as if saying *we're home*, the *darling*
held inside like dead
skin cells, afterthought.
Rain down the windows
trickle illogical shadows on the back
of the gloves. Had she been a man
they would have been
her honour. And now
she can't say she wants
them back. The knit is full of fissures.
In her grip, the nail clipper
appears to fornicate
with her fingertips:
she is undressing again,
sliding her silhouette
over the bed, accepting money.
A stray nail falls
on the top of the left glove,
like grappling hook.
Is she a thief reeling herself
towards the safe,
or a war prisoner intent
on escape? When she leaves,
she drops her gloves
at the feet of the night janitor.
She doesn't close
the door. Later, he looks inside
the motel room: on the floor,
a total of nine half-moons.

ii. Lawrence

So here is the glove
that he was. His departure is explicit,
a desecration of sorts. I touch
him in the secret places
where the leather, the stiff padding
have been burnt off.
His left hand had always
been weaker. And still it survived him,
survived the hose that escaped
his grip, the house,
the woman in the wheelchair
waiting to be saved. Why does everything
smell of God? The soot has left
my fingers looking
bruised. Two dead in the fire—
half of it him.
The glove is past bleeding now.
I cradle it like a gun
before pressing it to my temple.

iii. Mathilde

There's no viewing her hands.
The gloves burn white under the fluorescent light.
Several pearls have been sewed back on
inexpertly. The thread is lavender,
pulled taut and creating wrinkles on the silk.
In the end, even her eyesight
failed her, the floral
design fractured to a fault. And that was how
she was found: at the bottom
of the stairs, frozen in the act of clutching
a crucifix. How many bones did they have to break
to insert her hands in these gloves?
And there. How odd. The pain
has been taken from her—erased, like the husband
who chopped off her left index finger
when she tried to leave without telling him.
Someone has taken the trouble
to position her hands on her chest. In late prayer.
Her fingers, in clasping each other,
made to appear whole again.

Pandora

i

Under influence of heat,
paraffin returns to its liquid state.

Once the skin is dead,
it fails to recognise pain or the awareness
of pain. Skin is dependent
on breathing. Skin was, and now
it is a matter of watching
the brother wear a lipstick ten shades
brighter than the rest of the room.

This is she—going back to light the candle,
watch the flame eat its way through
the match to burn her fingers.

And by the time she comes
across the box, it is already open.

ii.

How long has this been going on?

A box jammed inside the room.
A trail of ants bearing down the wall.
Sadness under the fingernails
that leave even redder
streaks on the mosquito bite.

By candlelight, her hands
appear to have broken out of their bones.

And now the cat has declared
the corpse its boundary. Its paws
knead the new skin it occupies
as if taking notes, reading back the breath
that has gone out of the body.

She is counting the drip
of wax on her knuckles. Even the buttons
on the brother's shirt are numbered.

As if it is possible to place pain.
As if there is comfort in placement.
As if putting the body inside the box could
exile the silence when she brings
her ear against the wood.

She has barely begun
to rip out the runs in her stockings.

iii

And now she stops, like blood
painted on canvas—representational
and bereft of explanation.

She stands outside the box,
sees herself outside the room
that contains the box. She looks through
the window of the door
because it is proof
she can separate herself from the dead.

> (the cat licking the corpse's lips
>   the cat wearing the corpse's lipstick)

The digital watch's absence
has left a white scar around her wrist.

When she is old enough,
the brother said, she may be taught
how to control the fire,
how to watch the corpse feed its face to the light.

Her fear of the cat overshadows
her cheap shoes. It is only a matter of time
before the flame depletes the candle.

iv

She is growing blind,
and it is just as she imagined it—
the crushed mosquito,
the drinks, the blood overtones.

Steadily, the brother loses definition.
Her vision blurs into one cat,
one physical world
that is spilling from the box and rubbing
lipstick against her legs.

The smoke leaks of breath
gone bad. It is taking fifty-nine ants
to take the leg of a spider
halfway down the wall towards
deconstruction and continuance.

In the dark, she runs her hands
over the body, the cool skin that wraps
the face like a gift, the terrible
wrong done to the lips.

She is closing the lid.
Shutting the door behind her
with hands that she has learned to fear.
She is composed of many backs
turning away. How unhappy. This hope.

Seeing Birds in Church is a Kind of Adieu

The silence never lasts long.
Wings in the air stroke and turn it upside-down.
Ears were made to capture chaos,
you said. A tree sparrow raps
its beak on the pew as if to remind the wood
that it was once a tree. In my pocket,
five aluminium wrappers
without the candy. What is the stone floor
if not divisible by seating arrangement or shoes
that separate one person from another?
At the altar, a pigeon has found
the shoulder of Christ, its red feet
showing up like blood on the cracked marble.
How many did you feed with your eyes
as you lay dying? You wanted
a room that overlooked this church,
and now I'm inside it.
A blackbird observes the scene
from the bronze carving
of the 13th Station of the Cross.
At my right, an ornate window depicts a dove
in shards of coloured glass. It throws
a mottled light on my skirt,
like a corner of sun slipping out the door.

Refraction

There's a man in the kitchen, and it is afternoon.
Does the hour of death matter?
I let myself in. I have drizzle in my hair.
It is afternoon. His mouth is pressed on the tile
like a stethoscope. He is a study
on patience, on the heart's miscalculation
of its pocket universe. The window
illumines the hair on his legs.
It is afternoon. I've found my secret love.

And now I'm a flatline. The discoloured bathrobe,
in mothering his body, has washed
its purple dye under his nails.
I have death hiked up to my waist.
It is afternoon as the rest
of a woman's life can be an afternoon.
His left slipper drinks from the fallen Coke bottle.
His nothingness doubles into ants
on the counter. Between the body he is,
and the body he isn't, there's a refraction
of light. An afternoon, raised
like an arm reaching for the apple.

Inevitably

they closed the path through the woods.
In old woodpecker holes, squirrel

are dying. The local police knocked
on one door after another.

Illness makes the young lose balance,
dive headfirst into rabbit-holes.

Alice had been missing for days.
The urine of search-and-rescue dogs

permeates the grass. She was
last seen wearing her mother's clothes.

Too late, visitors are warned against
picking cyclamens, mushrooms.

Around the spot where she was
found, yellow lines play a strange

ring-a-ring o' roses. At night a Labrador
still howls, unsettles the peace.

All that remains of the body now
is a candy wrapper marked: *Eat me.*

Something Like Blood

Remember the tongue in your ear
at midnight, the smell of a brown
bag bursting because your favourite dog
is gone and the moon hangs
like a Frisbee on the blackwashed wall.

Yesterday morning your mother
came. The blue puppies on
the cereal box shook a premonition
on the coffee table: there'll be
an earthquake in five minutes,
rough little paws that scrape
asphalt in six, then hunger, like cats
on a brick wall, tails flicking
a fight for the carcass in the street.

In dreams you'll keep shouting: *Fetch!*
the way a handkerchief flaps in the wind.
This is the street where crows fly low
and the leash in your hand is a dead
weight, limp as the body under

the tires of her car. And she only
wanted to bring you fresh apple pie.

Seasonal Craving

Spring reawakens my urticaria for strawberries.
Where I come from, they are plump with formaldehyde,

embalmers have seasonal fruits in mind.
I see my brother's cerebral fluids stain the pillow.

The old Ford was smashed; the sound system
melted to black jam. The back wheels and fender

were stolen. Is anger the pip that stabs the crevice
between my teeth? I drowned crimson flesh

in grenadine while he sat across the table
and ordered a milkshake pink with crushed ice.

I still hear the blender behind the bar,
the coroner's saw whirling through his skull cap.

Strawberries taste of blood in my mouth, his lips
matted with a ridiculous shade of madder.

This is not the poem

you want to read
if you're looking for red squirrel,
found wisdom in stainless
pots, held hands
under a hot-air balloon.

The metre is uneven,
like the road to disco bars.
There was a time I called her
iambic because this was
how her small hand slipped
snugly into mine.

I choose my words with care:
she never liked my advice,
her etchings on the piano
grew fangs, we scheduled
the cat for therapy.

This is not the poem
you'll enjoy if you're after
a still life with apples.
Curious bystanders shouldered
each other to catch the last
scenes of that Saturday night.

Everyone was speechless.
Here's the sum of a girl's life:
mini-skirt, ecstasy, blue scooter,
shattered brick wall, blood on asphalt.
All bought with her allowance.

Ant trails

lead to the peach on the counter. It is overripe,
and your nail has left an open wound. Streetlight bathes

the kitchen into a shipwreck. A plate—chipped
in several parts—awaits the fruit, like proof of civilization.

With age, the tendency to live birthdays alone
ingrains itself in bone. Candles are stowed under the sink

for black outs. It is customary to collide against
the fridge in the absence of light. The dreamt-of pain

rubs against your knee, picking up on reality.
What is sleep, if not a finger pressing unconsciousness

upon the body? Something always drips out:
blood, juice, tears. The counter doesn't distinguish

your reflection from the fruit rot. After ten years,
it's still shining and—for the granite—it's enough to go on.

Once you've killed an ant, more arrive because
it is in the nature of workers to take the dead away.

Insomnia

It begins in loneliness,
in walking around the hospital

with a stethoscope.
You have twenty-six patients—

all of them your father.
A father is something you were

born with, like a port-
wine stain. A father may close

his eyes, but his heart
never sleeps—it is an orphanage

where children
produce rosary beads

around the clock.
You are an orphan now.

You have no one.
You have trained your ears

to hitchhike
in the heart of strangers—

and each beat reminds you
how afraid it is of stopping

Approaching Death

Uproot the camellias in the garden,
sweep away the fallen leaves whose ochre
stains permeate the grass. Forget
the French windows in the terrace,
how rust has eaten through hinges,
the hallway that leads upstairs.

Cover all the furniture, let white
sheets assume the flute music of ghosts.
Draw the curtains, switch on the lights:
books wait solemnly on shelves,
her Siamese cat disappears behind
the piano, a mud trail on the floor.

Wipe the mirror in the bathroom.
The sink is streaked with limestone
like crusts of salt on a cheek.
Unclog the drain and massage away
her fingerprints on the marble
counter imitating bruises.

Push aside the door to her room,
unhook abstract paintings from walls,
pick up magazines she kicked under the bed,
put away the medicine bottles on her
nightstand, listen to wind chimes
shiver a stream of notes from the porch.

Still the gurgling at her throat,
the fingers on her chest fidgeting
with lace. Settle down on the chair,
ignore the syringes, the stethoscope,
the IV drip. You hold her hand,
and it's just another rainy day.

Single Hung Window

Some days stillness permeates
the room. Like bay ghosts, they enter,
hands intertwined. Sunlight from
the window casts a rhombus on
the sideboard pushed against the sill.

The four-poster covets space
like a ship inside a bottle. Her daughter
follows the indolent dance of sailboats
through the glass pane, licks
dryness from her lips, imagines salt.

Her brother contemplates the reading
glasses on the table. Last winter
he learned how magnifying lenses
spark fire. His heart starts beating faster.
A day nurse blocks the threshold.

Immortality

The oak trees are nearer to it,
and they're not talking. Once our father

climbed one to retrieve a kite.
He found a nest littered with eggshells.

Be stuck or learn to fly, he said.
He had to break the string in several places

to get the kite down. Is the tree
any lonelier now without those birds?

It quickly refills with the activities
of squirrels. We tried covering his bedsores

with salve, but our father still seeped
out during the night. The hospital room

grew silent, like a tree. We emptied it,
and came home smelling too much of drink.

And Why Shouldn't I Cry Over Seinfeld?

It's a rerun, typical of summer.
My thumb finds the channel before it finds me.
I'm sitting on the same spot where
an old cat vomit left a map he called Antarctica.
A fruit fly buzzes the living room.
All of a sudden, I'm cold.
A nectarine slowly rots the fruit bowl.
I sneeze once, twice during the commercials.
I hear him again
saying he doesn't feel very well.
That night we only saw
a few minutes of the airing.
He never made it past the 8th season.
It's the first time I see Seinfeld alone.
I watch it for as long as I can.

In My Mother's Fridge

Suppositories congeal like foetuses
she couldn't have after a hurricane flew
the roof to Mexico. She has difficulty

swallowing when it comes to vegetables.
I find the broccoli settled against
the eggplants, decaying in the cold.

Through the years, we have learned to throw
away food, like pets that fail to survive
in the wild. A slice of cheese is pushed

into a corner, rye bread gathers mould
into its minuscule black holes.
Mineral water in a green plastic bottle,

laid sideways, drips over the tomatoes
and clarified butter. She admits feeling
immersed in bed. She has resigned

her wrist to the nurse's needle.
Overripe fruits bruise easily.
The odour of rotten lemons soaks

her room for months. For the most part
she is alone with picture frames: I am
the girl with braids, front-most to the left.

There was a red swing in the yard before
the chains broke and a gardener who tended
root crops. The potato in my hand peels

like the crust of tears around her eyes.
A draft enters through the space under the door,
tingeing her nails with the blues.

I won't ask you again

who that man is: clothed in white,
a thread trickling from the lapel—
he is your son, your father,
the brother you lost in the blood
between your mother's legs.

Here dusk is the twin of dawn.
And I'm holding your hands
like cold sand in ebb tide.
The sea spray tastes of your name.

This is how I'll remember
these last days: a dictionary
of symbols, the sistrum of Isis
on page 59, the morning sun
a rhombus on crumpled sheets.

Your mouth is dry. And words
prickle the tip of my tongue:
yesterday was porridge, tomorrow
will be fish, the world is flat.

I am the stethoscope curved
around the doctor's neck,
ice chips in a plastic glass.
And you, propped by pillows,
give in to the slow melt of death.

Surviving Grandfather

In the end, his fingers cast spidery
shadows on the wallpaper, white sheets
became stained: this was coffee,
everyone said, and we shouldn't stare.

At night we waxed candleholders
in the kitchen, and talked of courage:
it was swathed in silence, like military coffins
entering a chapel on the shoulders of men.

We were instructed to tiptoe, play
outside on sunny days. There was a dirt
path that led to the woods: the deal—
to return home before dark.

We wheeled our plastic dump trucks,
took the garbage out. Once a black bag
split open and spilled oversized
diapers, syringes, bottles on the grass.

Seconds passed, we froze:
this was not him coughing in the dark,
or one of our mothers at the piano
hesitantly stroking Rachmaninov.

First week of autumn, and he was gone.
We were back in school. That year we learned
the use of personal verb endings in Latin.

This is not the first time you tasted sand

There was a colonel
who glittered like the onyx
on your mother's finger.
The surrounding diamonds were
helicopters. He was caught
shouting orders when shrapnel flew.
For days afterwards you washed
brains down the drain. Someone
says there's luck in staying
all in one piece. Another complains
about overtime. Does picking up
the organs of another man mean
summer hibernates in the loose
pages of *Playboy* magazine?
Nightly you dream in stick figures:
the desert swarms with camels,
suicide bombers and maimed children
propped on Caucasian femurs;
enemies lie in the angles of
white stars. The analyst says
you've earned this vacation east
of Egypt. The sun has healing
properties when coupled by nurses
in short skirts. Here the women
are all headless, and your bed
in the morning is damp with urine.
No one returns totally whole.

5:37 p.m.

Arthur's hour of death was 5:37 p.m.
And now 5:37 p.m. is Arthur. I am powerless,
like when you fall asleep and the house
fails to exist. Every day I step into 5:37 p.m.
clapping my hands to announce
my presence. I am the intruder here.
My shoes turn inward the further I walk around
to retrieve paint that have peeled
from the ceiling. Receptacles, such as
pockets, are easily relieved of their emptiness.

I find myself playing the music
5:37 p.m. enjoys—the kind done in so many voices
that you forget you're actually alone.
While 5:37 p.m. is permanent and invariable,
I am a translation of events
that take place outside 5:37 p.m.
When I enter, it is in my substance
to remain in the background, vacillating—
a kind of muscle that could
at any time cease to function. Or Arthur
as he climbed to bed, then stopped breathing.

The Day She Was Called to Identify the Body

The windows crystallised late August:
still life with calendar, *Architectural Digest*.
The house wore heat like hosiery.
She took out a pack of tofu from the paper bag.
A gold pendant drummed against
her breastbone as tomatoes sliced themselves
from her hands. She thought in terms
of neon signs — the bars, the motel rooms,
the shops, the theatres that rolled
down streets like empty beer bottles.
The police grew in her hair
and reeked of runaway afternoon.
She said she didn't know who they wanted her
to think it was. She said, like that time
at the bus stop when he said he never wanted
to see her again, *This isn't my son*.
She gave them his age:
thirteen years, seven months and six days.
She stopped remembering anything else.

As we think

in circles, consider and reconsider
what to write on a marble slab,

our son's kidneys are swimming
the formaldehyde. This bottle

is the embalmer's kept woman,
and he hasn't been anyone

real in years. At some point,
a body stops breathing.

There's a certificate among
our valuables that underlines

a child's weight at birth.
We hold hands, count the words

we'd like to use. After twenty-six years
and seven weeks, the funeral is

ready in a day. The weather forecast
says partly cloudy, with brief

thunderstorms in the afternoon.
Does a tree feel pain

when it is split by lightning?
We look ahead, cross out numbers

on the calendar. The bed
in the middle of this room is

unruffled; we stand outside
the door like phantom limbs:

the windows have shut
on their own, and dust crawls

the shelves. His pen has rolled
into the swivel chair

and bled through the cushion.
Verdigris consumes the bronze frame

on his desk—his graduation
picture made to look watered down.

Like tea. Or an eye sinking
in the ocean of its own tears.

Hot tubs

gurgle like approaching storm,
or helicopters that hover over villages

before blades shatter from bullets.
Light through window grime

plays tricks over moving objects:
the ceiling fan rattles like dice

on a table, cockroaches
disappear into cracks on walls.

The Jacuzzi sputters like a drowning
lung: this is the way veterans relax.

In their youth, they claimed
the future lay in napalm and laughed.

Years later in Saigon,
the wristwatches of dead soldiers

glitter from shop windows, like eyes
before that flash of shrapnel.

Leopold's Room

Your throat catches, but you film on.
The unmade bed appears less real then the ants
collecting crumbs from the sheets:
the cheese cake has survived its eater
and lies forgotten in the fridge.
As a child, Leopold stole furniture
from the dollhouse of his girlfriend, Sheila.
When his mother found out,
she made him take everything back
and never told anyone. It could be because
she was lonely herself.
You wonder if she still keeps
a derringer for protection. You kick the slipper
with its vomit stain under the night
stand. What Leopold
really desired were the dolls,
Sue and Francine, because of their hair.
He could refuse to share your spoon and tell you
he loved you. *When a patient starts*
coughing up blood, the nurse said,
it's time to move on. She had pretty hair.
She was Sheila again for Leopold;
he was 16 to her. Now
his mother wants him back. With pictures
of his room. You can be
who you want to be because
neither you nor he will be part of it.
The curtains—craggy with nicotine—billow,
smudging a view of the lake.
The tape jams. You don't slap
the video camera awake, but watch
the wind shut the closet door on Leopold's secrets:
the x-rays, the synthetic wigs,
the unworn sweaters
with moth holes mouthing sarcomata.

The Ventriloquist Returns

He hasn't changed. He's still
wearing the shirt he used to wipe

between his mother's thighs
after she died. He's holding a baguette

the way he would shake hands
with a prosthesis. The screen door closes

halfway behind him: he is again
in the study of parts. He brings inanimate

things to life with his voice—
as if the whole world could be stuffed

into a parrot and ease the pain of having
a shoulder. He takes off his shoes,

and his feet pick up dust
as he walks. The windows are streaked

with mud and cracked in several places.
When it rains, the house appears

to weep from the inside. Sometimes
he smells her urine in his breath.

Today sunlight bleeds
—pond-green and diaphanous—

through dirt like tadpoles
or stomach lining. The walls

are a wreckage of silence.
Hamsters in their cage momentarily

look up and stop fornicating.
He is doomed in knowing the exact

words his mother would use
to survive a grief like his.

Dollhouse

To go through the furniture,
I've had to pry open three walls.
I notice the kitchen first because a slice of tape
holds the cupboard shut.
After her son died,
Aunt Claire replaced the dining table
with a Titian carpet: six chairs
positioned in a circle—as if awaiting
the apocalypse or signalling its absence.
It is, in part, her grief.
I imagine her fingerprints
as they became superimposed
on the surface of everything she touched.
The miniature chandeliers
have burnt out their bulbs, like tulips
left on a grave to wilt.
The still life paintings hang
crookedly as if bent into materialising
her solitude—in this dollhouse,
there is no room for dolls.
I've seen the interior, now I close it.
She's gone,
save for the desire
to keep inside just a little longer
every appearance of living.

Winter Elements

There's a woman in room 46D,
and bedsores that gape from blankets.
We live in the constant gurgle
at her throat where names rise like
genies, their powers snuffed out long ago.

The sponge baths are tepid, mattresses
soiled after a period of incontinence,
table sugar like prayer beads over wounds.
In-between massages, our hands
meet halfway, fingertips briefly
touching at the curve of her spine.

In this ward, patients have pupils
dilated from morphine. Last night she lost
her ability to swallow while turkey
thawed in the kitchen and the nutritionist
told Polish jokes over the gravy sauce.

We never celebrate the holidays,
or converse in more than a whisper.
On sunny mornings I draw the curtains,
change the water in the vases.
You empty her urine bag down the toilet.
Sometimes I hear you cry.

Outside snow settles, like her body
on the bedspread. By the window,
yesterday's bouquet wilts,
the cheap pine table freezing
under the white petals of camellias.

Mrs D's Last Letter to Her Son

Beware of the woman who starts her sentences
with darling, or pauses halfway through

the door with *You got a light?* She lives
in smoke, drinks heavily on weekends,

studies the capabilities of spongy matter
in captivity, admires the geometric cigars

of Seymour Lipton while drinking iced tea
in a plastic cup. Her breasts are cold sugar lumps,

the cream deftly withheld up to the last moment.
Bone is in her eyes, like tunnels where fog

rises between 11p.m. and midnight.
She lacks foresight when it comes to raising

children, sitting with a spindle in the room
and smoking two packs of Gauloises a day.

Remember the needles, the rendezvous with
nurses, butterflies on her wrist. They say

a body can squeeze itself into a lung,
shed hair like loose pages and survive on throat rot.

She is nothing but trouble, a pre-defined dig.
You pay to have her name etched in stone.

This closing book

is the loft window flying from its hinges
into the eye of a hurricane, the envelope

your sister slashed with a metal knife
and never answered, the briefcase chained

to a dead man's wrist. For no apparent
reason, the blender jams like a blues

musician inside a glass paperweight.
Some days you watch a quartered apple

turn brown and forget the missing pieces
on your chess set. Truth is you never read

the instructions on how to bait the white
queen with a black bishop or why the safety

latch unscrews in time. At a flutter
of the afterword, soldiers disappear,

horses kick the barn door open. There are
letters that remain etched deeply in

your palm, the vowels shaped like prickly
pears. These are not one of them, and

you are not holding the correct warranty
for this product. Documents are easily

misplaced between pages 13 to 59, the weather
subject to misinterpretations like elephants.

At this hour, the ventriloquist is in bed.
His recurrent dream: this book closing.

Death in the Afternoon

Walk slowly.
Enmesh yourself in the crowd.

> Gnats lay eggs on his face—
> on the dumbstruck eyes,
> in the rolled-up mouth.

You hear murmured:
Coronary thrombosis. Indigestion. Even constipation.

> Sirens weave into open space.
> Gnats disperse. The ones left behind
> are zipped up in a black disposal sack.

A gnat settles on you
and you suffocate with it—or wish you did.

> The bags are packed. Back doors open and close.
> Actors are spirited away. The show is over.
> No credits given.

When you leave the crowd—
don't ask for your money back.